Know Your Freshwater Fishes

GW00482338

Know Your Freshwater Fishes

Dr Mark Everard

First published 2016

Copyright © Mark Everard 2016

Published by
5M Publishing Ltd,
Benchmark House,
8 Smithy Wood Drive,
Sheffield, S35 1QN, UK
Tel: +44 (0) 1234 81 81 80
www.5mpublishing.com

A catalogue record for this book is available from the British Library

ISBN 978-1-910456-20-0

Book layout by Servis Filmsetting Ltd, Stockport, Cheshire
Printed by Replika Press, India
Photos as credited

Acknowledgments

The author would like to thank all those who have given permission to use their photographs throughout this book to supplement my own images. Also to my friends at Old Pond Publishing for excellent support and high-quality production of what I hope will be an informative and enjoyable guide.

Contents

Introduction

Often, the eye does not penetrate the surface film of a body of water. This is a shame, as the freshwater flora and fauna of the British Isles is both diverse and spectacular. The freshwater fishes comprise the most charismatic group of organisms living out their lives underwater in Britain, occupying a range of habitats. The fresh waters of the British Isles are diverse, ranging from torrential hill streams to powerful rivers and wide, meandering lowland channels. Canals and drainage channels, varying in size from ditches to the large Fenland drains of eastern England also hold fishes, as do reservoirs, lakes, ponds and other stillwater bodies.

Adaptations and characteristics of freshwater fishes

All of Britain's freshwater fishes breathe by passing water across gills, swim using fins and lay eggs. However, beyond this common feature, the body form of fishes often betray their preferred habitats and life habits. For example, fishes adapted to stronger flows – such as dace and trout – have streamlined body forms. Others better adapted for more control in sluggish or still waters, such as common bream, tend to have deeper bodies that are also more strongly flattened flank to flank. Fins also betray much of the life habits of fishes. For example, the dorsal (back), anal (rearmost of the fins on the underside) and tail fins of pike are located close together at the rear of the fish, providing it with the propulsive power to accelerate explosively to ambush prey. The pectoral (behind the gills) and ventral (beneath the belly) fins are paired, and are well-developed in fishes like the tench, providing more precise control during slow, gentle swimming as the fishes forage for edible items on the bed of still or slowly flowing waters.

The position, size and other features of the mouth too reveal much about the life habits of the fish. Bleak and rudd, for example, have mouths that are turned upwards, better suiting them to feeding from or near the water's surface. By contrast, the mouth of barbel, gudgeon and the loaches is angled downwards, equipping them for life on the bed. Other fishes, such as chub and roach, have mouths positioned centrally, enabling them to readily exploit food items across a range of depths. The mouths of predatory fishes, such as pike and zander, are large and armed with teeth to help them hunt fishes and other live prey.

The bodies of most species of British freshwater fishes are covered in scales, bony overlapping plates providing both armour and flexibility. The presence or absence and the number of scales varies between fish families and species, and can be helpful in distinguishing between similar fish species. This is particularly true of the number of scales along the lateral line: a series of sensory pits along the flanks of most groups of fish.

A wide range of books is available for those seeking more detailed information about Britain's freshwater fishes, including:

- Everard, M. (2013). *Britain's Freshwater Fishes*. Princeton University Press/WildGUIDES, Princeton.
- Maitland, P.S. (2004). *Keys to the Freshwater Fish of Britain and Ireland, with Notes on their Distribution and Ecology*. Freshwater Biological Association Scientific Publication No.62. The Freshwater Biological Association, Ambleside.

British freshwater fish families

The fish fauna of the British Isles comprises not merely a diversity of species – 54 species including a number that are not truly freshwater residents but can be found in estuaries and lower reaches of rivers – but also fishes from 21 different families with quite different characteristics. The fishes in this guide are grouped according to the most common families.

The **carp and minnow family** *(Cyprinidae)* is most strongly represented in the British freshwater fish fauna, including 12 native species and seven additional species that have been introduced. The cyprinids have toothless jaws, bodies covered evenly by scales (excepting some scaleless, artificially reared strains), and a single dorsal fin supported by soft rays behind fused spines at the leading edge.

The **salmon, trout, charr, freshwater whitefish and grayling family** *(Salmonidae)* is the next best-represented family, including seven native species (one of which is considered extinct) and two introduced species. These salmonids have a slender, streamlined body shape adapted for fast swimming, with a fleshy adipose (or fatty) fin set towards the rear of the back. The jaws are armed with a single row of sharp teeth (except the grayling).

The **perch family** *(Percidae)* is represented in the British Isles by three species, two of which are native and one introduced. The percids possess two dorsal fins, the front one supported by strong spines.

The **lamprey family** *(Petromyzontidae)* is represented in British waters by three relatively scarce native species. The bodies of lampreys are superficially eel-like with a cartilaginous skeleton, no scales or paired fins, and a mouth without jaws but which comprises a circular disk.

The **stickleback and tubesnout family** *(Gasterosteidae)* comprises two native British freshwater species. The bodies of these small fishes are elongated, lacking regular scales though covered by scutes (large bony scales) along the sides, with the front dorsal fin modified into a series of well-developed spines.

The **herring, shad, sardine and menhaden family** *(Clupeidae)* includes two British species that live their adult lives in the sea but spawn in freshwater rivers.

A number of families are represented by just one species each in British fresh waters, including the **pike family** *(Esocidae)*, the **sculpin family** *(Cottidae)*, the **loach family** *(Cobitidae)*, the **river loach (or hillstream loach) family** *(Balitoridae)*, the **hake and burbot family** *(Lotidae)*, the **freshwater eel family** *(Anguillidae)* and the **sturgeon family** *(Acipenseridae)*.

Other fishes introduced to British fresh waters come from families such as the **North American freshwater catfish family** *(Ictaluridae)*, the **sheatfish catfish family** *(Siluridae)* and the **sunfish family** *(Centrarchidae)*.

Fishes from some other families are primarily marine, but may move into estuaries and can venture up into the lower reaches of rivers particularly during the summer, so are considered briefly towards the end of the book. These include three species from the **mullet family** *(Mugilidae)* and one each from the **temperate bass family** *(Moronidae)*, the **righteye flounder family** *(Pleuronectidae)*, the **smelt family** *(Osmeridae)* and the **silversides family** *(Atherinidae)*.

Photographic credits

Glossary

Alevin.   The first larval life stage to emerge from the egg, the larva still largely undeveloped and attached to a yolk sac.

Ammocoete.   The freshwater, larval life stage of lamprey species.

Anadromous.   Fishes that live their adult lives in the sea or estuaries but return to fresh waters to breed.

Brackish.   Saline water generally found in estuaries that is not as fully saline as seawater.

Carnivorous.   Diet that comprises mainly animals.

Crepuscular.   Active at dusk and dawn.

Gill rakers.   Filamentous bony or cartilaginous extensions from the gills, generally used for filtering fine food particles from the water.

Glacial relics.   Fish adapted to cold waters, often found as scattered populations in deep lakes, presumed to be relics of a colder glacial period of history.

Holarctic.   The northern regions of America, Greenland and Eurasia.

Invasive.   A species introduced beyond its native range that can establish self-sustaining populations potentially threatening the balance of ecosystems.

Natal.   Place where something is born or, in the case of British freshwater fish species, hatched.

Naturalised.   A species introduced beyond its native range that becomes established as a viable breeding population.

Omnivorous.   Eats a variety of plants, animals and amorphous organic matter.

Ovipositor.   A tube growing from the vent of some female fish (bitterling in breeding condition) through which they deposit eggs.

Parr.   The longest-lasting freshwater stage of a migratory salmon, between the fry stage and the smolt.

Piscivorous.   Eats fish.

Redds.   Depressions cut into the gravel of river or lake beds, generally by female fish of the salmon family or by lampreys to deposit eggs.

Smolt.   The phase of a salmon or sea trout's life in which it takes on a silver sheen, migrates down the river and metamorphoses into the sea-going adult form.

Zooplankton.   Small animals suspended in the water column.

Roach

(Rutilus rutilus)

Other common names: Redfin
Family: Carp and minnow
Location: Throughout the British Isles
Size: Up to 50cm (20in), 1.8kg (4lb)
Habitat: Rivers and still waters
Status: Native

The roach is one of the most widespread species of British freshwater fish, adapted to life in both standing and flowing waters. Roach are omnivorous, juveniles feeding extensively on small invertebrates and algae and older fishes tending towards a more plant- and detritus-based diet. Roach can be found in powerful rivers, small streams, canals and ponds as well as large lakes and estuaries, reflecting their adaptability to a range of conditions and diets.

Roach spawn in shoals on submerged vegetation from April to early June, depending on conditions. There is no parental care.

Roach have a deep, laterally compressed body covered evenly in large, conspicuous scales (42 to 45 along the lateral line). Body colour is generally silver, darker on the back and pale beneath, with bright red fins. The mouth lacks teeth and barbels.

Roach are often confused with rudd, a primary distinguishing feature being that the leading edge of the dorsal fin is in line with that of the ventral fins.

Rudd

(Scardinius erythrophthalmus)

Other common names: None
Family: Carp and minnow
Location: Throughout the British Isles
Size: Up to 50cm (20in), 1.8kg (4lb)
Habitat: Still waters and slower rivers
Status: Native

Rudd are found primarily in standing waters, though also in slow flowing rivers, often inhabiting middle and upper layers. Mature rudd in food-rich waters can take on a vivid golden and crimson coloration. However, rudd are prone to over-breeding in small still waters, resulting in dense populations of stunted fishes lacking bright colours.

Rudd spawn communally on submerged vegetation in the spring, the sticky eggs receiving no subsequent parental care. Young rudd feed extensively on small invertebrates, becoming increasingly omnivorous as they grow.

Rudd have a deep body profile with an even covering of large, conspicuous scales over a generally golden-silver body colour and crimson fins, the mouth lacking teeth and barbels.

Rudd are often confused with roach. Primary distinguishing features are the leading edge of the dorsal fin, which is set back 2–3 scale columns from that of the ventral fins, and an upturned mouth.

Chub

(Squalius cephalus)

Other common names: Chevin, loggerhead
Family: Carp and minnow
Location: Throughout mainland Britain
except the far north and west
Size: Up to 60cm (24in), 6.7kg (10lb)
Habitat: Rivers, but can survive in still
waters
Status: Native

Chub are common fishes of flowing waters, although they can survive and grow large (though not breed) in large standing-water bodies. They can live for up to 20 years.

Chub spawn in shoals on river gravels in late spring or early summer, with no parental care once eggs are laid. The fry require warm, shallow marginal water to enable them to grow quickly enough to withstand winter spates. Cool summers with poor growing conditions often lead to the loss of most of the juveniles by year end, resulting in strong and weak year classes in chub populations. Juveniles feed on algae and small invertebrates. Older fishes become increasingly omnivorous as they grow – plants, fish, amphibians and other small animals all make up the diet.

Chub have a streamlined but 'chubby' profile, rounded in cross section and with an even covering of large, brassy and conspicuous scales. The dorsal and tail fins are dark, and the ventral fins reddish. The mouth is large, lacking teeth and barbels.

Chub are often confused with dace. However, the outer borders of the dorsal and anal fins of chub are convex, whilst those of dace are concave.

Dace

(Leuciscus leuciscus)

Other common names: Dare, dart
Family: Carp and minnow
Location: Throughout mainland Britain
except the far north and west
Size: 40cm (16in), 0.6kg (1.5lb)
Habitat: Rivers
Status: Native

Dace are common in flowing waters, particularly those of good quality, across the British Isles and much of northern Europe. They are active at all depths of the water column including taking food items from the surface, particularly during warmer months.

Dace spawn communally on river gravels in late winter or early spring, depositing sticky eggs that receive no parental care. Juveniles exploit the spring boom of available food, adaptation to cold conditions means that dace continue to feed and grow throughout the year. Young dace require food-rich warm water in river margins to maximise growth during their first summer. Adult fishes remain omnivorous but preferentially feed on larger invertebrates and fish fry.

Dace have slender, streamlined bodies covered evenly in large, conspicuous scales (48–51 along the lateral line). Body colour is generally silvery, darker on the back and pale or white beneath, with pale fins. The mouth lacks teeth and barbels.

Dace are often confused with chub. However, the outer borders of the dorsal and anal fins of dace are concave, whilst those of chub are convex.

Orfe

(*Leuciscus idus*)

Other common names: Ide, golden orfe
Family: Carp and minnow
Location: Localised populations in a few southern rivers, sporadic garden pond escapes elsewhere
Size: Up to 85cm (33in), 4kg (8.8lb)
Habitat: Rivers
Status: Introduced, locally naturalised

Orfe occur naturally in still and slowly flowing fresh waters across central and north-west continental Europe and Asia. Though not native to the British Isles, orfe have been widely introduced, primarily due to releases from the ornamental fish trade, and have become naturalised in some places such as the River Mole in Surrey.

In their native range, orfe migrate up tributary streams to spawn communally on gravel or submerged vegetation in early spring. The sticky eggs receive no parental care. Juvenile orfe feed on algae and small invertebrates and tend to be gregarious. Larger orfe progress to a diet comprising mainly insect larvae, other invertebrates and, opportunistically, fish fry.

Orfe have relatively small but conspicuous scales (56–61 along the lateral line). The outer edges of the dorsal and anal fins are convex, the tail is forked and the mouth lacks teeth and barbels.

In its natural form, the body colour is generally silvery, paler beneath and darker on the back. However, a 'golden' form, popular in garden ponds, is better known.

Common Bream

(Abramis brama)

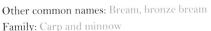

Other common names: Bream, bronze bream
Family: Carp and minnow
Location: Throughout England, particularly
in lowlands and more nutrient-rich areas
Size: Up to 82cm (32in), 9kg (20lb)
Habitat: Still waters and slow-moving rivers
Status: Native

The common bream is a widespread shoaling species found in still and slow-flowing waters. Their diet is omnivorous, the high back and compressed sides adapting them to grub around for invertebrates and other food in soft sediment.

Common bream spawn communally in the late spring or early summer, shedding eggs on submerged vegetation and exhibiting no parental care. Juvenile common bream feed extensively on small invertebrates, older fishes tending to have a more varied diet, feeding primarily on the bed of the river or lake. The body colour changes with age: silvery in younger fishes but darkening to bronze with age.

Common bream have high backs and strongly laterally compressed flanks covered in large scales. The mouth lacks teeth and barbels, but can be protruded to help the fish suck up food from the river bed.

Common bream can be confused with silver bream, but have 51–60 scales along the lateral line, a mouth that can be protruded and a smaller eye.

Silver Bream

(Blicca bjoerkna)

Other common names: White bream, bream flat

Family: Carp and minnow

Location: Naturally in lowland south-east England

Size: Up to 36cm (14in), 0.6kg (1lb 5oz)

Habitat: Still waters and slow-moving rivers

Status: Native

Silver bream occur in still and slow-flowing waters, typically near the bed, where they shoal and feed.

Silver bream spawn communally during the late spring or early summer on submerged vegetation, often with a few discrete spawning events, releasing sticky eggs and exhibiting no parental care. Juveniles grow rapidly, feeding extensively on small invertebrates, whilst older fishes tend to have a more omnivorous diet.

Silver bream have deep, laterally compressed bodies evenly covered with conspicuous scales, and colourless fins. The mouth lacks teeth and barbels, and the large eye is typically a quarter the diameter of the head.

Silver bream can be confused with common bream, but have 44–48 scales along the lateral line, a mouth that does not protrude into a tube, and a larger eye.

Barbel

(Barbus barbus)

Other common names: 'Beard', 'whisker'
Family: Carp and minnow
Location: Naturally in rivers draining to the North Sea from the Humber to the Thames systems, but more widely introduced across England and some of Wales
Size: Up to 120cm (47in), 9kg (20lb)
Habitat: Larger rivers with stronger flows
Status: Native

Barbel are robust fishes of flowing waters, opportunistically omnivorous and inhabiting the lower layers of water where they feed on the river bed.

Barbel spawn communally over well-flushed gravels during late spring or early summer, often disturbing the gravel bed into which their sticky eggs may fall, offering a little protection though there is no parental care. Juvenile barbel feed on small invertebrates, though growing barbel adopt a more omnivorous diet that includes any animal and plant matter they can root out from the river bed using their sensitive barbels and strong, fleshy lips. As the British Isles are at the extreme northern extent of the barbel's European range, spawning does not automatically occur and neither is fry survival assured, with slow growth during cooler summers.

Barbel have
streamlined bodies
covered in bronze
or olive scales, with
strong, amber fins –
the pectorals are well
developed – adapted for
life on river beds. The
mouth is underslung,
lacking teeth but with
strong, fleshy lips and
two pairs of barbels
used to locate food.

Juvenile barbel may
be confused with
large gudgeon, but
possess two pairs of
barbels rather than the
gudgeon's single pair.

Tench

(Tinca tinca)

Other common names: Doctor fish
Family: Carp and minnow
Location: Throughout the lowlands of the
British Isles
Size: Up to 70cm (28in), 6.8kg (15lb)
Habitat: Still waters and sluggish rivers and
drains
Status: Native

Tench are adapted to life in weeded still or sluggish waters, grubbing in soft sediments for plant and invertebrate food items.

Tench spawn communally over dense vegetation in rapidly warming shallows during late spring or early summer when the water reaches 18°C. Groups of male tench, distinguished from females by their spoon-shaped ventral fins, chase and jostle gravid females. The female tench release many small, green, sticky eggs, which adhere to water plants but which thereafter receive no parental care. Warm, shallow water is essential for the growth of juvenile tench, which feed extensively on a range of invertebrate and algal matter. Young tench remain cryptic, living in dense vegetation as they grow, adult fishes graduating to an omnivorous diet.

Tench have a characteristically olive-green or occasionally brown coloration, fading to yellow beneath, over a rounded body shape. The flanks are smooth to the touch due to a dense covering of small scales overlain with a thick, gelatinous slime. The fins are rounded and the eyes small and red.

The small mouth, which can be protruded to aid feeding, lacks teeth but has a single barbel at each corner.

Crucian Carp

(*Carassius carassius*)

Other common names: Crucian, carassin (French)
Family: Carp and minnow
Location: Mainly southern England
Size: 64cm (25in), 3kg (6lb 10oz)
Habitat: Still waters, ideally well vegetated
Status: Native

Crucian carp are a small native carp that generally remains well hidden in vegetated waters. Initially native to the eastern side of England, it is now more widespread across the British Isles through introductions. Crucian carp tolerate low oxygen conditions, high temperatures and prolonged ice cover, and can thrive in densely vegetated pools and marshes, though compete poorly with other species in open waters.

Crucian carp spawn in the late spring through to the summer, females shedding small, sticky eggs into dense vegetation in shallow water. There is no subsequent parental care. Juvenile and adult crucian carp feed on small animals and plant matter throughout their life.

Crucian carp frequently interbreed with both common carp and wild goldfish, posing a conservation threat.

Crucian carp have notably humped backs, evenly covered with conspicuous scales over a brassy or olive-coloured body. The mouth is small and lacks barbels. The dorsal fin is long with a strong, slightly serrated third spine preceding the soft rays.

Hybrids with common carp are usually betrayed by the presence of barbels. Hybrids with the very similar goldfish are difficult to determine, and best left to experts.

Goldfish

(Carassius auratus)

Other common names: Brown goldfish
Family: Carp and minnow
Location: Scattered throughout the British Isles
Size: Up to 32cm (13in), 1.8kg (4lb)
Habitat: Still waters and sluggish rivers
Status: Introduced

Goldfish are small, hardy carps native to the still waters of central Asia, China and Japan, but have been introduced widely across the world, mainly through the ornamental fish trade. Wild populations of goldfish revert to their natural, bronze colour form, very similar in appearance to the crucian carp with which they interbreed. Goldfish are hardy, tolerating poor water quality, and are well adapted for life in small ponds or thickly vegetated pools and marshes.

Goldfish spawn communally when the water temperature exceeds 20°C, females releasing small, sticky eggs that adhere to water plants and receive no parental care. Juvenile and adult fishes feed on small animals and plant matter throughout life.

Goldfish share many of the features of the crucian carp, including a notably humped back, an even covering of conspicuous scales, and a lack of barbels around the mouth. Ornamental varieties of goldfish come in orange and other colours, some with modified fins, but wild populations revert to the natural bronze colour.

Hybrids produced when goldfish interbreed with crucian carp and common carp possess intermediate features and are difficult to identify.

Common Carp

(Cyprinus carpio)

Other common names: King carp, koi, leather carp, mirror carp
Family: Carp and minnow
Location: Throughout the British Isles
Size: Up to 110cm (43in), 27kg (60lb)
Habitat: Still waters and lowland rivers
Status: Introduced, naturalised

Common carp are amongst the largest freshwater fishes in the British Isles, introduced here in successive waves from at least the 15th century through their hardiness, omnivorous habits and consequent uses for aquaculture, sporting purposes and, in their artificially reared coloured forms, as ornamental fish. The voracious, omnivorous diet, fast growth and large size, and habit of grubbing up sediment can make common carp problematic through disrupting aquatic ecosystems, often profoundly.

Common carp spawn communally over dense vegetation from late spring to summer when the water reaches 18–20°C. Male fishes chase and jostle gravid females, which shed small, sticky eggs that adhere to submerged vegetation but receive no parental care. Common carp are omnivorous with voracious appetites throughout their life cycle.

Common carp occur in various forms and colours due to selective breeding. The natural form is high backed and elongated, covered evenly with conspicuous scales of a brassy colour. The dorsal fin is single and elongated. Two pairs of short barbels surround a toothless mouth that may be protruded to aid feeding.

Hybrids produced when common carp interbreed with crucian carp and goldfish possess intermediate features, also generally distinguished by small barbels around the mouth.

Gudgeon

(Gobio gobio)

Other common names: 'Trent barbel', goby
Family: Carp and minnow
Location: Throughout mainland Britain but mainly southern and western areas
Size: Up to 20cm (8in), 140g (5oz)
Habitat: Rivers and some still waters
Status: Native

Gudgeon are small, bottom-dwelling, bottom-feeding fishes widely distributed throughout mainland Britain. They are sometimes confused with juvenile barbel. They tend to shoal on the bottom, feeding opportunistically on a range of small plant, animal and other organic matter.

Gudgeon spawn communally from late spring to early summer, usually when water temperature approaches 15°C, doing so in shallow water on gravel or vegetation. Eggs are released at intervals over several days, sticking to submerged surfaces but receiving no parental care. Juvenile gudgeon feed extensively on small invertebrates and algae, older fishes feeding opportunistically on the river bed on a range of small food items.

The scales of the gudgeon are prominent and pearlescent, the flanks mottled with an iridescent overlay. The body is streamlined and flattened beneath, reflecting adaptation to life on the river bed. The fins are colourless but have some dark mottling. The underslung mouth lacks teeth, and a single barbel is present at each corner.

Gudgeon are distinguished from small barbel by their single pair of short barbels.

Grass Carp

(Ctenopharyngodon idella)

Other common names: White amur
Family: Carp and minnow
Location: Where stocked throughout the British Isles
Size: Up to 150cm (59in), 45kg (99lb)
Habitat: Still waters
Status: Introduced, non-breeding

Grass carp occur naturally from China to eastern Siberia in still waters, large rivers and brackish waters across a wide temperature range (0–38°C). The species was initially introduced to the British Isles to control aquatic weeds, as it has a pronounced herbivorous diet. As grass carp are not known to breed in British waters, the species persists here solely through stocking, which today is mainly for ornamental and angling purposes.

Grass carp spawn in their native regions on river beds with very strong currents and at relatively high temperatures of 20–30°C, the eggs drifting in the current. The requirement for high temperatures and long rivers are factors leading to the failure of grass carp to breed in British rivers.

Grass carp have an elongated, cylindrical body evenly covered with prominent scales and of an overall bronze to olive colour that fades to paler beneath. The snout is short and the mouth is terminal, lacking barbels or teeth.

Minnow

(Phoxinus phoxinus)

Other common names: Penk
Family: Carp and minnow
Location: Throughout mainland Britain
Size: Up to 14cm (6in), 20g (0.7oz)
Habitat: Rivers and well-oxygenated still
waters
Status: Native

Minnows are small, shoaling fishes that thrive where the water is fresh and well oxygenated, both in rivers and in the turbulent margins of large bodies of standing fresh water.

Minnows spawn in shoals on the marginal gravels of rivers and large lakes multiple times throughout the summer. During spawning, male and female minnows often form discrete shoals that come together to spawn. Males become spectacularly gaudy, developing white patches at their fin bases and with a kaleidoscope of emerald, red and gold colours across the body, females retaining their overall silver-brown colouration. The eggs and fry receive no parental care. Juvenile minnows feed extensively on small invertebrates and algae. Growing and adult fishes feed opportunistically on a wide range of small food items, including invertebrates and plant matter.

Minnows appear scaleless, but are evenly covered with fine scales and smooth skin. The streamlined body, rounded in section, is brown on the back and silver or white beneath, with a prominent black line formed from a series of overlapping 'dots' running the length of the body along the midline. The fins are small, rounded and colourless, the small mouth lacking teeth and barbels.

Bleak

(Alburnus alburnus)

Other common names: 'River swallow'
Family: Carp and minnow
Location: Throughout the British Isles
Size: Up to 25cm (10in), 170g (6oz)
Habitat: Rivers
Status: Native

Bleak are small fishes of flowing waters, found in the upper layers of rivers where they sometimes form dense shoals. Bleak are omnivorous and feed primarily at the surface. Juveniles feed extensively on small invertebrates and algae, whereas older fishes feed opportunistically on small food items, particularly invertebrates, borne on the current or the water's surface.

Bleak spawn during the spring on stones, gravel or nearby vegetation in shallow water, the sticky eggs receiving no parental care.

Bleak have prominent scales, generally silvery in colour, but are darker and commonly greenish on the back. The body is streamlined and laterally compressed and the large mouth and eyes are both upwardly pointing, reflecting the species' surface-feeding habit. The fins are colourless, and the base of the anal fin is particularly long. The mouth lacks teeth or barbels.

Bitterling

(Rhodeus sericeus)

Other common names: Bitterling carp
Family (both fish): Carp and minnow
Location: Pockets throughout England
Size: Up to 11cm (4in), 16g (0.6oz)
Habitat: Still waters and slow river margins
Status: Introduced, locally established

Small fishes, not native to Britain, bitterling were introduced through aquarium releases, becoming locally naturalised with strongholds in south Lancashire, Cheshire, parts of Shropshire and some of the Great Ouse catchment. Nowhere are bitterling abundant, but imports are now controlled to avert future problems. Their favoured habitat is densely weeded regions of still waters and slow-flowing river margins with sandy or muddy bottoms where freshwater mussels occur. Bitterling have an omnivorous diet.

Bitterling spawn in a unique way. Males develop bright body colouration and select a mussel, to which they attract females. Gravid females have a long ovipositor tube through which they deposit eggs into the mollusc's mantle cavity via its siphon tube. Fertilised eggs attach to the mussel's gills, safe from predators, free-swimming fry later emerging via the mussel's siphon tube.

Bitterling have deep, laterally compressed bodies with a short lateral line that peters out five or six scales behind the gill covers. The silver flanks contrast with the grey-green back, and a distinct metallic stripe extends from the middle of the flank to the base of the tail. The mouth is small, pointing forwards or slightly to the underside of the blunt snout.

Atlantic Salmon

(Salmo salar)

Other common names: Salmon, 'king of the fishes'

Family: Salmon, trout, charr, freshwater whitefish and grayling family

Location: Cleaner rivers particularly to the north and west

Size: Up to 150cm (59in), 29kg (64lb)

Habitat: Rivers, estuaries and open sea

Status: Native

Atlantic salmon live their adult lives at sea, returning after 1–4 years to their natal rivers to spawn.

Salmon run rivers from late winter to the autumn, arriving at open gravel-bedded headwater reaches in early winter. Gravid females cut redds into gravel patches defended by males. Their non-sticky eggs fall into crevices, hatching in the spring. Hatchlings, known as alevins, still have yolk sacs attached. Alevins remain in the gravel until the yolk is consumed, then swim up as fry to feed on small invertebrates. Fry develop into parr, distinguished by a series of 'dirty fingerprints' along the flanks. Parr feed on invertebrates for 1–3 years before metamorphosing into silvery smolts that run down rivers to the sea to begin their adult, predatory lives.

Atlantic salmon have silvery, streamlined bodies, their large eyes and mouth adapted to life as fast-swimming predators. Mature males develop a kype (hooked lower jaw) as a weapon to defend spawning sites.

Unlike brown/sea trout, the salmon's mouth does not extend behind the eye. Salmon also generally lack spots below the lateral line, and have a pronounced 'wrist' before the tail fin.

Brown Trout

(Salmo trutta)

Other common names: 'Brownie', fario
Family: Salmon, trout, charr, freshwater whitefish and grayling family
Location: Throughout the British Isles, particularly in cleaner and clearer rivers and large lakes
Size: Up to 140cm (55in), 30kg (66lb)
Habitat: Faster rivers and large still waters
Status: Native

Brown trout are so adaptable that they were originally classified into many different species. The sea-going sea trout form described on the following page can grow considerably bigger than freshwater forms, which do not approach the maximum stated size for the species. Trout have considerable commercial value for recreational angling and aquaculture.

Brown trout breed in cool, well-oxygenated rivers, lake-dwelling trout running tributary rivers to spawn. Male trout guard territories over suitable gravels in autumn or early winter, gravid females cutting one or more redds and depositing non-sticky eggs which fall into the gravel's pores to hatch in late winter or early spring. Alevins emerge from the eggs with yolk sacs still attached, swimming up as fry when the yolk is consumed. Fry and parr feed on aquatic and terrestrial invertebrates and small fishes.

Brown trout are salmon-like, with a streamlined body, small head, large mouth and short, strong teeth. Body colouration varies with habitat, many freshwater trout having buttery-brownish flanks with spots of varying colours.

Unlike rainbow trout, brown trout have 3–5 spines on the leading edge of the dorsal and anal fins, and lack a pink or red stripe along the flanks and spots on the tail.

Sea Trout

(Salmo trutta)

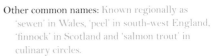

Other common names: Known regionally as 'sewen' in Wales, 'peel' in south-west England, 'finnock' in Scotland and 'salmon trout' in culinary circles.

Family: Salmon, trout, charr, freshwater whitefish and grayling family

Location: Throughout the British Isles, in coastal waters and cleaner and clearer rivers and lochs

Size: Up to 140cm (55in), 30kg (66lb)

Habitat: Coastal seas, estuaries and faster rivers

Status: Native

Sea trout are a sea-going form of brown trout, with considerable commercial value for recreational angling.

The sea trout life cycle is similar to that of the Atlantic salmon, adults running rivers to breed in cool, well-oxygenated headwaters. Male sea trout guard territories over suitable gravels in autumn or early winter, gravid females cutting one or more redd and depositing non-sticky eggs which fall into the gravel's pores. Alevins, with yolk sacs still attached, hatch in late winter or early spring, emerging from protective gravels as fry when the yolk is consumed. Fry and parr feed on invertebrates and small fishes, metamorphosing into smolts, which run to coastal seas or estuaries for a marine adult life phase spanning one or more winters.

Sea trout are salmon-like in terms of their silvery body colour as well as their streamlined form, with a small head and large mouth with short, strong teeth.

Sea trout have a larger mouth than Atlantic salmon, extending behind the eye, and tend to have spots below the lateral line. They lack a pronounced 'wrist' before the tail fin.

Rainbow Trout

(Oncorhynchus mykiss)

Other common names: Rainbow, blue trout, steelhead
Family: Salmon, trout, charr, freshwater whitefish and grayling family
Location: Throughout the British Isles, mainly as a stocked fish
Size: Up to 120cm (47in), 25.4kg (60lb)
Habitat: Rivers and still waters, mainly where stocked
Status: Introduced, rarely naturalised

Rainbow trout occur naturally in rivers flowing into the Pacific along the west coast of North America from Alaska to Mexico, where they also have a sea-going form: the steelhead salmon. However, rainbow trout have been widely introduced across the temperate world for aquaculture and recreational angling. A few populations are known to be self-sustaining in the British Isles, but most rainbow trout originate from stocking from trout farms. Rainbow trout are predators, feeding on aquatic and terrestrial invertebrates and small fishes.

Rainbow trout generally undertake short spawning migrations into suitable streams with a clean gravel bottom, male fishes defending territories and female fishes cutting redds, into which they deposit eggs that are not then guarded. The life cycle is typical of other members of the salmon family.

Rainbow trout have a streamlined body and a jaw lined with fine, strong teeth.

Principal features distinguishing rainbow trout from brown trout include the absence of spines on the leading edge of both the dorsal and anal fins, and the presence of the characteristic wide pink or red stripe running along the flank from head to tail.

Brook Trout

(Salvelinus fontinalis)

Other common names: American brook trout

Family: Salmon, trout, charr, freshwater whitefish and grayling family

Location: A few scattered high-altitude lochs on the west coast of Scotland

Size: Up to 86cm (34in), 9.4kg (21lb)

Habitat: Isolated Highland lochs

Status: Introduced, rarely naturalised

Brook trout have been introduced to British waters over a number of years, but have only become naturalised in a few scattered high-altitude lochs on the west coast of Scotland. Larger, sea-running strains are found in the native range (the east coast of Canada and USA), accounting for the large maximum size reported above. However, brook trout encountered in the British Isles are generally small, but voracious in exploiting the sparse fare of invertebrate and fry food sources.

Brook trout undertake short spawning migrations to suitable reaches of stream or lake margins with a clean gravel bottom, male fishes defending territories and female fishes cutting redds, into which they deposit eggs that are not guarded. The life cycle is typical of other salmon family members.

Brook trout have the streamlined body and jaw lined with fine, strong teeth typical of members of the salmon family.

The dorsal and anal fins lack spines at their leading edge, and the flanks are characterised by a combination of dark green marbling on the back and dorsal fin and by red spots with blue halos on the flanks.

Grayling

(Thymallus thymallus)

Other common names: 'Lady of the stream'
Family: Salmon, trout, charr, freshwater
whitefish and grayling family
Location: Throughout mainland Britain in
strongly flowing, clean rivers
Size: Up to 50cm (20in), 1.8kg (4lb)
Habitat: Strongly flowing, clean rivers
Status: Native

Grayling are shoaling river fishes that feed on invertebrates foraged from the stream bed or surface. Curiously, grayling have an odour often likened to fresh thyme, from which their scientific name derives.

Unlike other members of the salmon family, grayling spawn in the spring. Like other salmonids, males defend territories on well-flushed gravel beds and females deposit unguarded eggs. At spawning time, male grayling darken and intensify in colour, becoming aggressive to other males in defence of territories. Male fishes hold their spectacular, iridescent blue-red dorsal and pelvic fins erect to display to females, enticing them to dig redds and lay eggs. Grayling generally spawn communally, though with discrete territories within the overall spawning area. Juvenile grayling are fast growing. These fishes are not long lived.

Grayling are distinctive in appearance, with an elongated, streamlined body. Their flanks are silvery and iridescent, dappled with irregular dark spots interspersed with hints of purple, green and copper. They have soft toothless jaws. The 'sail-like' shape of the large dorsal fin, particularly enlarged and coloured in male fishes, is characteristic.

Their graceful appearance leads to their common nickname of the 'lady of the stream'.

Arctic Charr

(Salvelinus alpinus)

Other common names: Char, 'torgoch' (Wales), 'tartan-fins'

Family: Salmon, trout, charr, freshwater whitefish and grayling family

Location: Deep, well-oxygenated glacial lakes to the north and west of the British Isles

Size: Up to 107cm (42in), 15kg (33lb)

Habitat: Deep glacial lakes

Status: Native

Arctic charr occur across northern North America, Europe and Asia. They are a cold-adapted species occurring only in deeper waters of large, deep lakes of the northern and western British Isles, and are considered a glacial relict species left behind as glaciers retreated following the last Ice Age. Arctic charr are extremely sensitive to pollution and are of significant conservation concern across their remaining British range. Sea-going forms of Arctic charr are found across its global range, but British populations are restricted to fresh waters and are considerably smaller than the maximum stated size for the species.

Arctic charr enter tributary rivers or migrate towards well-flushed lake margins during autumn or winter, when water temperatures reach around 4°C, spawning in well-oxygenated gravel beds. Schooling behaviour is abandoned at these times, mature males becoming territorial in their defence of ideal spawning gravels over which they coax gravid female fishes to cut their redds and deposit their eggs.

Arctic charr share many characteristics of the salmon family, with an elongated, streamlined body and a small head and large mouth adapted for a mobile, predatory lifestyle.

Unlike brown trout, Arctic charr have teeth only in the central forward part of the mouth. The body colour of Artic charr varies dramatically with habitat, different strains once considered separate species.

The Whitefishes

European Whitefish *(Coregonus lavaretus)*
Vendace *(Coregonus albula)*
Houting *(Coregonus oxyrinchus)*

Other common names:
- **European whitefish:** These vary by region including powan (in Loch Lomond), schelly or skelly (in Haweswater, Ullswater and Red Tarn in the English Lake District), gwyniad (in Llyn Tegid [Lake Bala] in Wales) and pollan (in Northern Ireland)
- **Vendace:** European cisco
- **Houting:** None

Family: Salmon, trout, charr, freshwater whitefish and grayling family
Location: Deep lakes in formerly glaciated regions of the British Isles
Size: Up to 46cm (18in), 0.9kg (2lb)
Habitat: Deep, well-oxygenated glacial lakes
Status: Native

The whitefishes are part of a separate sub-family *(Coregoninae)* of the salmon family. They have small mouths and weak teeth. Like Arctic charr, they are considered as glacial relics.

European whitefish and vendace occur in deep, well-oxygenated lakes across the north and west of the British Isles. These species breed during the winter on marginal gravels around lake shorelines when the water is about 6°C. Fry and adults feed largely on invertebrates, sometimes rising up in the water column to feed by night. Populations are vulnerable to pollution particularly by organic matter that suppresses oxygen levels. They are also threatened by the introduction of ruffe and other small fishes preying on eggs and fry.

The houting, with its characteristic long, pointed snout, is now considered extinct.

European whitefish typically have a laterally compressed, spindle-like body with a bluish or dark green, often very dark back. The head is conical, with a small ventral mouth. The tips of the pectoral and pelvic fins are dusky and the dorsal, anal and tail fins are dark, large and conspicuous compared to the smaller fins of the closely related vendace (shown), which also has a deeply forked tail.

Pike

(Esox lucius)

Other common names: 'Freshwater shark'
Family: Pike
Location: Throughout the British Isles
Size: Up to 130cm (51in), 27kg (50lb)
Habitat: Rivers, still waters and estuaries
Status: Native

Pike are large fishes found in both running and still waters including the upper reaches of estuaries. They are predatory, ambushing other fishes (though they also seek out dead fishes) as well as amphibians and small aquatic mammals and birds. They have pronounced cannibalistic tendencies.

Pike spawn early in the year, from late February to May depending on conditions. Large female pike move into vegetated backwaters or shallows generally accompanied by several smaller male pike. Large females commonly devour the smaller male fishes that assemble around them before spawning. Sticky eggs adhere to vegetation and receive no parental care. Juvenile pike are predatory from the fry stage, exploiting the fry of later-spawning fish species as well as their siblings.

The scales of the pike are numerous and small, the flanks usually mottled green to provide camouflage.

The pike's lifestyle as an ambush predator is further aided by its large eyes and cavernous mouth armed with sharp teeth, and anal and dorsal fins set to the rear of its streamlined, muscular flanks enabling rapid acceleration. The rounded fins are supported by soft rays.

Perch

(*Perca fluviatilis*)

Other common names: European perch
Family: Perch
Location: Throughout the British Isles
Size: Up to 60cm (24in), 2.7kg (6lb)
Habitat: Rivers and still waters
Status: Native

Perch are distinctive predatory fishes common in both standing and still waters across the British Isles, including the upper reaches of estuaries. Perch commonly shoal, and are often found near sunken branches and other vegetation from where they launch predatory raids. Shoals of hunting perch often betray their presence at dusk as shoals of small prey fishes 'explode' at the surface to evade these raids.

Perch spawn communally on hard, submerged surfaces in the spring, the eggs and fry receiving no parental care. Juveniles feed predominantly on small invertebrates, progressing to a diet of larger invertebrates, amphibians and fishes as they grow. Stunted populations of perch can occur in small still waters where they breed prolifically but outstrip food resources.

Perch have bold, black stripes on their greenish, rough-scaled flanks. They have two dorsal fins, the front strongly spined and the rear with soft rays. The large mouth lacks barbels, and the jaws lack teeth.

Perch may be confused with ruffe, but are distinguished by their vertical stripes, separation between the dorsal fins, and a black spot to the rear of the first dorsal fin.

Ruffe

(Gymnocephalus cernua)

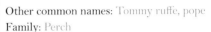

Other common names: Tommy ruffe, pope
Family: Perch
Location: Naturally southern and eastern
and central England but spreading
Size: Up to 20cm (8in), 170g (6oz)
Habitat: Rivers and still waters
Status: Native, spreading through
introductions

Ruffe are small, shoaling fishes of standing and flowing waters across mainland Britain. Many populations beyond their native range in lowland southern, central and eastern England result from introductions.

Ruffe spawn in shoals in shallow water during the spring. Females deposit their eggs, which receive no parental care, in sticky strands that adhere to vegetation and stones. Juvenile ruffe eat small invertebrates, with progressively larger animal prey items taken as the fishes grow.

Introductions of ruffe into some waters where they are not native have resulted in serious threats to species of conservation concern, such as gwyniad and vendace, due to the ruffe predating their eggs and fry.

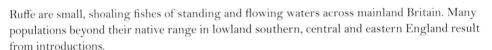

Ruffe are generally silvery in colour with two dorsal fins, the front spiny and the rear with soft rays. The scales are small and the fins translucent. The large mouth lacks barbels, and the jaws lack teeth.

Ruffe may be confused with small perch, but lack strong vertical stripes on their flanks. Unlike perch, the ruffe's two dorsal fins are connected.

Zander

(Sander lucioperca)

Other common names: Pike-perch
Family: Perch
Location: Throughout the Ouse, Thames and Severn river systems with range still spreading
Size: Up to 100cm (39in), 9kg (20lb)
Habitat: Rivers, still waters and upper estuaries
Status: Introduced, locally naturalised

Zander are a predatory species introduced to Britain from mainland Europe, and their range is still spreading from its southern and eastern England origins. Zander are found in both still and flowing waters of adequate depth, where they subsist as largely crepuscular or nocturnal predators feeding primarily on other fishes. As an introduced predator, the zander has the potential to perturb British freshwater ecosystems, so further introductions are discouraged.

Zander spawn in late spring or early summer when water temperatures exceed 12°C, laying sticky eggs on hard substrates that may include rocks, plant stems and underwater tree roots. Male fishes clean the spawning substrate and guard the eggs and newly hatched fry. Juvenile zander feed on zooplankton and other invertebrates, progressing to a mainly piscivorous diet.

Zander possess two dorsal fins, the front supported by spines and rear by soft rays with a distinct gap between these fins. The flanks are generally silver with a greenish tinge, covered in small scales.

The eyes are distinctively large and reflective, aiding hunting in low light. The jaws are armed with teeth but lack barbels, and the inner surface of the mouth is rough.

Wels Catfish

(Siluris glanis)

Other common names: Catfish, moggie, whiskers
Family: Sheatfish catfish
Location: Localised waters mainly in southern England
Size: Up to 500cm (197in), 306kg (675lb)
Habitat: Still waters and sluggish large rivers
Status: Introduced, locally naturalised

The wels catfish, native to fresh and brackish waters of western Asia and continental Europe, has been introduced and locally naturalised in some southern still waters of the British Isles. Wels catfish are generally inactive by day, hiding in cover, but emerge as voracious nocturnal predators that feed in warmer months on almost any fishes, fowl or mammal prey.

Wels catfish breed in early summer in vegetated margins of lakes and large rivers, laying eggs on mounds of leaf litter which are guarded by the male catfish. Juvenile wels catfish are superficially similar to tadpoles, but grow rapidly in warm water, feeding on a variety of invertebrates and progressing to a wholly carnivorous diet.

Given their large size and voracious appetites, further introductions of wels catfish are unwise.

The wels catfish has a cavernous mouth, three pairs of long barbels or 'whiskers', tiny widely spaced eyes and a body that tapers away like a giant tadpole.

Body and fin colour is dark, generally a mottled grey, but paler beneath. The dorsal fin is small, lacking spines, but the anal fin is very long.

Stone Loach

(*Barbatula barbatula*)

Other common names: Loach, stoney, beardie, groundling
Family: River loach (or hillstream loach)
Location: Throughout the British Isles except Scotland
Size: Up to 13.5cm (5.5in), 20g (1oz)
Habitat: Rivers and streams, rarely lake edges
Status: Native

Stone loach inhabit running waters including small streams and, occasionally, the shorelines of lakes. They are secretive by day, concealing themselves under stones and dead wood on sandy, muddy or stony bottoms, and generally nocturnal, when they emerge to feed primarily on small invertebrates. Adult fishes are largely solitary, though favourable refuges may harbour other loaches as well as bullheads.

Stone loach spawn in the spring, females shedding clusters of sticky eggs amongst gravel, submerged stones and plants. Females have sometimes been reported guarding the eggs. Habitat in which to hide is important for the growth and survival of this secretive fish.

Stone loach are elongated and scaleless, colour varying with habitat but usually dull yellow-brown with irregular blotches. The fins are rounded, the dorsal fin set to the rear of the body. Six barbels surround the mouth, two pairs beneath the tip of the snout and one pair at the corners of the mouth.

Stone loach may be confused with spined loach, but have longer barbels and lack backward-pointing spines beneath the eyes.

Spined Loach

(*Cobitis taenia*)

Other common names: Loach, spiney, groundling

Family: Loach

Location: Catchments of the rivers Trent, Great Ouse, Welland, Nene and Witham in eastern England

Size: Up to 13.5cm (5.5inches), 30g (1oz)

Habitat: Rivers and slow-moving drains

Status: Native

Spined loach are one of Britain's smallest and rarest native fishes, almost entirely restricted to a few catchments in eastern England. Spined loach are not highly mobile, living in dense submerged vegetation where they remain by day. Spined loach emerge by night to feed on small bottom-living invertebrates as well as some vegetable matter.

Spined loach spawn in spring, depositing unguarded eggs on submerged plants, roots or stones. The fry are very small, and the generally small size of adults too necessitates dense vegetation for survival and reproduction.

Spined loach are elongated and strongly laterally compressed, with minute scales and light brown colouration with 19 brown spots along the flanks. Three pairs of short barbels surround the small mouth, and a strong, retractable double-pointed spine is located in a skin pouch below and in front of each eye.

Spined loach may be confused with stone loach, but the spines below the eyes are diagnostic and the barbels are much smaller.

Bullhead

(Cottus gobio)

Other common names: Miller's thumb, bullyhead, mullyhead, wayne
Family: Sculpin
Location: Throughout mainland Britain
Size: Up to 10cm (4in), 20g (0.7oz)
Habitat: Rivers and streams, rarely lake edges
Status: Native

Bullhead are small fishes, the only freshwater member of their family. They are found on the gravel or rocky bed of rivers and the wave-lapped edges of larger still waters. Bullheads are flattened on the underside and lack a swim bladder, living out their solitary lives in 'caves' beneath rocks or woody debris that may constitute their territory for life. Bullheads are exclusively carnivorous, feeding on invertebrates and fish fry.

Bullheads spawn during the spring, male fishes enticing neighbouring females into their territorial caves to deposit around 100 sticky eggs in clusters, generally on the cave's ceiling. After fertilising the eggs, the male drives off the female and then nurtures the eggs through to hatching, caring for the fry until they venture out to locate and establish their own territories.

The bullhead is so named for its large and broad head, with a big mouth and a pair of small eyes positioned on the top.

Bullheads have a mottled brown body that tapers away behind with two dorsal fins, the front dorsal fin shorter with spines and the rear one soft, and a long anal fin beneath. A large pair of mottled pectoral fins matches body colouration.

Common Sturgeon

(Acipenser sturio)

Other common names: Sturgeon
Family: Sturgeon
Location: Throughout the British Isles
Size: Up to 6m (20ft), 400kg (880lb)
Habitat: Rivers and estuaries
Status: Native

The common sturgeon is, in fact, anything but common, though possibly one of the commonest of the increasingly scarce 23 species within the sturgeon family found across the Northern Hemisphere. The common sturgeon is a scarce and generally solitary visitor to British waters, and is now considered on the verge of extinction.

All sturgeon are anadromous, inhabiting marine waters and returning to freshwater rivers to breed. Little is known about the marine phase, but mature fishes enter rivers to breed. Female common sturgeon deposit 800,000 to 2,400,000 small dark, sticky eggs at each spawning on sand, gravel and stones. Juveniles return to estuaries and the open sea, growing slowly and maturing after seven to nine years. Some specimens can live as long as 100 years.

The body of the common sturgeon is elongated, with five rows of large armoured scales, known as scutes, along each side. The mouth is small, toothless and protractile, located beneath the snout and with four barbels between it and the elongated snout. The back is olive-blue, fading to paler on the underside.

Burbot

(Lota lota)

Other common names: Mariah, 'the lawyer', eelpout
Family: Hake and burbot
Location: Considered extinct in the British Isles
Size: Up to 152cm (60in), 34kg (75lb)
Habitat: Sluggish rivers and still waters across the Holarctic
Status: Extinct in Great Britain (but frequent across northern Eurasia and America)

The burbot is the only member of this otherwise marine family to be found in fresh water. Although it has a wide distribution in lakes and slow-flowing waters across northern America and Eurasia, the burbot is now considered extinct in the British Isles, though unsubstantiated rumours of its continued existence persist.

Burbot spawn in the winter, often under ice, with mature fishes migrating into shallow margins to spawn communally at night on sand or gravel beds. The tiny eggs, one to three million released by each female, contain an oil globule enabling them to float off into the water column. Many die, but those that survive produce minute burbot fry that feed on small planktonic animals, progressing to larger invertebrate prey as they grow.

The burbot's unusual 'cod-like' appearance reflects the marine ancestry of its family. The elongated, mottled body has two soft dorsal fins, the second of which is long, and a rounded tail and long anal fin. There is a single barbel beneath the large mouth.

Shad Species

Twaite Shad (*Alosa fallax*)
Allis Shad (*Alosa alosa*)

Other common names: None
Family: Herring, shad, sardine and menhaden
Location: Anadromous fishes spawning in a few
western rivers

Size:
- **Twaite shad:** Up to 60cm (24in), 1.5kg (3.3lb)
- **Allis shad:** Up to 69cm (27in), 4kg (8.8lb)

Habitat: Selected fast and clean western rivers,
and estuaries
Status: Native

Twaite shad and allis shad are similar, both increasingly uncommon in British rivers, to which they return to spawn, though living their adult lives as schooling marine fish. Both shad species feed on small fishes and crustaceans of a size that matches the fishes as they grow.

Both shad species migrate up rivers in the spring to spawn in large shoals by night in fresh running water over sand or gravel bottoms, the allis shad reported to do so at higher temperatures (22–24°C) than the twaite shad (10–12°C), though this is contradicted by conditions in the British rivers in which they spawn. Spawned fishes return to the sea, fry progressively moving downriver to reach estuaries during their first summer.

Shad are herring-like with large, round scales and minute teeth.

Twaite shad (shown) have a dark spot behind the gill with 7–8 spots along the flank, and gill rakers shorter than the gill filaments.

Allis shad also have a dark spot behind the gill but none along the flank, and the gill rakers are nearly or as long as the gill filaments.

Three-spined Stickleback

(Gasterosteus aculeatus)

Other common names: 'Prickleback', stickybag
Family: Stickleback and tubesnout
Location: Throughout the British Isles
Size: Up to 11cm (4in), 20g (0.7oz)
Habitat: Rivers and still waters including small water bodies and brackish waters
Status: Native

Three-spined sticklebacks are small and hardy, tolerant of significant pollution, and occur in river edges, small streams and ditches, farm ponds and the margins of large still waters, where they can form dense shoals. In some rivers, particularly spate rivers, three-spined sticklebacks overwinter in estuaries or coastal waters. This stickleback is carnivorous, feeding on small invertebrates and fish fry.

During spring, male three-spined sticklebacks become brightly coloured and territorial, building nests of vegetation glued together using secretions from their kidneys. Males then attract females with a characteristic 'zig-zag' dance, driving them off after their eggs are laid and repeating the process with three or four different females. Males become devoted fathers, fanning water through the nest, removing dead eggs, and caring for the fry for a few days after they become free swimming.

Three-spined sticklebacks have streamlined, laterally compressed bodies armoured sparsely with large scales, known as 'scutes'. Colour varies with season, male fishes developing emerald flanks and a red breast during mating, while females remain browny-silver.

The first dorsal fin is reduced to three prominent spines, distinguishing it from the similar ten-spined stickleback, which has 9–10. The eyes are large and the mouth is small, lacking barbels.

Ten-spined Stickleback

(Pungitius pungitius)

Other common names: Nine-spined stickleback
Family: Stickleback and tubesnout
Location: Throughout the British Isles except northern Scotland
Size: Up to 11cm (4in), 20g (0.7oz)
Habitat: River edges, small streams and still waters
Status: Native

Ten-spined sticklebacks are small, occasionally shoaling fishes that inhabit river edges, small streams and still waters, but are intolerant of brackish water. They favour well-vegetated habitats, so are somewhat more restricted in range than the three-spined stickleback. Ten-spined sticklebacks feed mainly on small invertebrates and fish fry.

In spring or summer, male ten-spined sticklebacks become brighter in colour and establish territories within which they construct nests of vegetation glued with secretions from their kidneys. Breeding males attract females using a distinctive 'zig-zag' dance; females are then driven away after depositing their eggs in the nest. Male sticklebacks guard the eggs, fanning water over them, removing dead ones, and protecting the fry for a few days once they become free swimming.

Ten-spined sticklebacks have the same elongated, laterally compressed form as three-spined sticklebacks, but are more streamlined and of a more regular dull or silvery colour.

The first dorsal fin is reduced to the 9–10 prominent spines, giving the species its common name and distinguishing it from the similar three-spined stickleback, which has only three. The mouth is small, lacking barbels, and the eyes are large.

European Eel

(Anguilla anguilla)

Other common names: Eel, snig
Family: Freshwater eel
Location: Throughout the British Isles
Size: Up to 91cm (36in), 5.4kg (1 lb)
Habitat: Rivers, still waters and estuaries
Status: Native

European eels can live either in saline or fresh water. They can evade detection, burying in soft sediment or inhabiting caves or dense vegetation, becoming actively predatory by night.

The eel has a remarkable life cycle. Eggs assumed to be laid in the Sargasso Sea produce flattened larvae that drift for two years on the Gulf Stream, arriving on European shores, whereupon they metamorphose into transparent 'glass eels'. Some remain in coastal waters and estuaries, whilst others ascend rivers and other water bodies including streams, lakes, reservoirs, ponds and ditches, even travelling over land on wet nights. Late in the year, often on dark nights with new moons and after as much as 20 years, maturing eels turn silvery and run back down rivers to sea to complete the cycle.

The eel's snake-like body appears superficially scaleless, yet is covered in minute scales under a coat of thick slime, making the fish smooth to touch and difficult to hold.

The dorsal fin runs most of the length of the body, joining with the caudal (tail) fin and the anal fin. Ventral fins are absent, but the pectoral fins are well developed. Eels have a large mouth, which lacks barbels.

Brook Lamprey

(Lampetra planeri)

Other common names: Planer's lamprey, European brook lamprey, 'nine eyes', pride, sandpride or brookie

Family: Lampreys

Location: Throughout the British Isles except the far north of Scotland

Size: Up to 20cm (8in), 57g (2oz)

Habitat: Rivers

Status: Native

The brook lamprey is a small, eel-like fish. Lampreys are not technically true fishes as they lack jaws, scales and paired fins, and also have a cartilaginous skeleton.

Unlike the other two British lamprey species, brook lampreys do not migrate, but live as ammocoete larvae for several years in silt in the edges of streams and the headwaters and margins of rivers, remaining buried and inconspicuous and filter-feeding or grazing on detritus.

After several years, brook lamprey ammocoetes metamorphose into adults that are initially shorter than their larvae, developing an eel-shaped body and two contiguous dorsal fins. Adult brook lampreys do not feed, instead spawning communally in river gravels soon after metamorphosis and dying shortly thereafter.

Ammocoetes, rarely longer than 15cm (6in), are toothless and blind with little pigmentation. The two dorsal fins merge into the tail fin.

Adults are eel shaped, slightly metallic in colour, with a pair of functional eyes and a small sucking disc with blunt, weak teeth. The seven small, round gill openings on either side of the head were once thought to be additional eyes.

River Lamprey

(Lampetra fluviatilis)

Other common names: Lampern, juneba, stone grig, lamper eel
Family: Lampreys
Location: Throughout the British Isles except the far north of Scotland
Size: Up to 50cm (20in), 150g (11oz)
Habitat: Rivers and estuaries
Status: Native

The river lamprey has a similar life history to the brook lamprey to the point of metamorphosis from the ammocoete, after which the river lamprey grows on and migrates down river to live out its adult life in the estuaries of large rivers as a parasite. River lampreys attach themselves to the sides of other fishes, feeding on their flesh and body fluids rasped off with circular rows of teeth in the mouth disc.

Mature river lampreys run rivers to spawn in late spring or summer, adults working in pairs or groups to move stones to create spawning depressions into which sticky eggs are laid. There is no parental care, adults dying shortly after spawning.

Ammocoetes, rarely longer than 15cm (6in), are toothless and blind with little pigmentation. The two dorsal fins merge into the tail fin.

Adults develop a round, disc-shaped mouth lacking jaws and a cartilaginous skeleton. The drab, slate-grey or brownish body lacks scales and paired fins. Behind the pair of functional eyes are seven small round gill openings either side of the head.

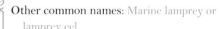

Sea Lamprey

(Petromyzon marinus)

Other common names: Marine lamprey or
  lamprey eel
Family: Lampreys
Location: Throughout the British Isles but
  mainly England and Wales
Size: Up to 120cm (47in), 2.5kg (5lb 8oz)
Habitat: Rivers, estuaries and marine
Status: Native

The sea lamprey has a similar life history to the brook lamprey to the point of metamorphosis from the ammocoete, though the sea lamprey ammocoete is bigger and more strongly coloured. After metamorphosis, the sea lamprey migrates down river to live out its adult life in the sea. Here, the sea lamprey lives as a parasite, attaching to and rasping off flesh and body fluids from prey fishes with circular rows of teeth in its jawless mouth disc.

Mature sea lampreys run rivers to spawn in late spring or summer, adults working in pairs or groups to move stones to create spawning depressions into which sticky eggs are laid. There is no parental care, adults dying shortly after spawning.

Ammocoetes, rarely longer than 15cm (6in), are toothless and blind. The two dorsal fins merge into the tail fin. Sea lamprey ammocoetes have extensive black pigmentation.

Adults have a round, disc-shaped mouth lacking jaws, a cartilaginous skeleton, a large pair of functional eyes, and lack scales and paired fins. Seven small round gill openings are found on either side of the head.

North American Interlopers

Pumpkinseed *(Lepomis gibbosus)*
Black Bullhead *(Ameiurus melas)*

Pumpkinseed:
- **Other common names:** Pond perch, sunny
  Family: Sunfish
- **Size:** Up to 20cm (8in), 180g (6oz)

Black bullhead:
- **Family:** North American freshwater catfish
- **Size:** Up to 66cm (26in), 3.6kg (7lb 11oz)

Location: Pockets throughout England
Habitat: Still waters and calm river margins
Status: Introduced, locally established

Two North American fishes occur in English waters, released from the ornamental fish trade. The import of both is now banned due to their potential to establish and disrupt aquatic ecosystems.

- Pumpkinseed sunfish were introduced to mainland Europe and the British Isles in the 1890s as aquarium fishes and for use in research, becoming established locally from Somerset to as far north as County Durham. Pumpkinseeds have a predatory diet. Their high fecundity enables dense populations to become established.
- Black bullheads are related neither to the native bullhead nor to the introduced wels catfish. They have become widely introduced across Europe, where they can form dense populations. Black bullheads are voracious and omnivorous, potentially outcompeting other species and eating their spawn and juveniles.

Pumpkinseed sunfish (above) have electric-blue highlights across the flanks and strong blue, green and red colouration around the head. The dorsal fin is long, consisting of a spined front fin fused into a soft-rayed rear fin.

Black bullheads (below) have a black, scaleless body. They possess eight barbels and are armed with three long, sharp spines, one each on the leading rays of the pectoral and dorsal fins.

Invasive Alien Species

Topmouth Gudgeon *(Pseudorasbora parva)*

Sunbleak *(Leucaspius delineatus)*

Family (both fishes): Carp and minnow
Location: Pockets throughout England
Top-mouth gudgeon:
- **Other common names:** Stone moroko, clicker barb
- **Size:** Up to 11cm (4in), 16g (0.6oz)

Sunbleak:
- **Other common names:** Belica, motherless minnow
- **Size:** Up to 25cm (10in), 170g (6oz)

Habitat: Rivers and still waters
Status: Alien, invasive

Two small fishes introduced to British freshwater and now locally established have become problematic. Their rapid growth rate to adult size, capacity to breed after only their first year, multiple spawnings on leaves or stones throughout the spring and summer, protection of eggs by male fishes, and tendency to eat the spawn of other fishes enables them to rapidly colonise new waters, outcompeting native species.

- Topmouth gudgeon are native to flowing and still freshwaters from Japan to the Amur basin, feeding on invertebrates, fishes and fish eggs.
- Sunbleak are shoaling surface-feeding fishes from areas of Asia and Eastern Europe, favouring slow-flowing and still waters.

Topmouth gudgeon (upper image) have an elongated, spindle-like body covered in prominent scales. The fins are not significantly elongated at the base. The snout is slender, the mouth oriented upwards, and a prominent longitudinal pigmented line extends along the flank.

Sunbleak (lower image) are bright silver in colour, easily identified by the incomplete lateral line that peters out shortly before the end of the pectoral fin.

Estuarine Residents

Sand-smelt *(Atherina presbyter)*
European Smelt *(Osmerus eperlanus)*
Flounder *(Platichthys flesus)*

Location: British estuaries particularly around the south and west
Habitat: Estuarine, occasionally lower rivers
Status: Native

Several fish species inhabiting estuaries and coastal seas can penetrate the lower reaches of rivers, particularly during the summer months. Three of the commonest are:

- The sand-smelt, also known as the sparling or little sand-smelt, is a member of the silversides family (Atherinidae). Sand-smelt are a small, shoaling inshore species favouring estuaries and entering lower reaches of rivers, feeding on zooplankton (small animals in the water column).
- The European smelt is not related to the sand-smelt, belonging instead to the smelt family (Osmeridae).
- The flounder is a member of the righteye flounder family (Pleuronectidae). It is the only species of British flatfish that enters fresh waters. Flounder can penetrate considerable distances up rivers. Both eyes are normally on the right side of the body, hence the family name.

Sand-smelt have an intense silvery line, often outlined in black, from head to tail along a silvery, laterally compressed body covered in relatively large scales.

Smelt (shown) have a pointed head and snout, the lower jaw reaching to the hind margin of the eye, and a single dorsal fin.

The pigmented upper side of the flounder's body changes colour to match muddy and sandy bottom sediments. The fins lack spines.

Marine Fishes that Visit Estuaries

European Seabass
Mullet Species

Location: British estuaries particularly around the south and west

Habitat: Estuarine, occasionally lower rivers

Status: Native

Several primarily marine, sea-spawning fishes occupy British estuaries, particularly during summer months, including:

- European seabass *(Dicentrarchus labrax)*, a predator.
- Thick-lipped grey mullet *(Chelon labrosus)*, the thick upper lip of which is wider than half the eye diameter.
- Thin-lipped grey mullet *(Liza ramada)*, the upper lip of which is always less than half as wide as the eye diameter.
- Golden grey mullet *(Liza aurata)*, with a small mouth, long pectoral fins that fold forwards past the rear of the eye orbit, and a distinctive golden spot on the gill cover.

All four fishes move northwards and inshore with warming weather, often penetrating brackish and fresh waters, retreating during cold conditions. The mullets are schooling fishes that graze algae and other organic matter with their rubbery lips.

European seabass (top) have elongated bodies, silvery-grey/bluish on the back and silver on the flanks. The front-most of their two dorsal fins comprises 8–10 sharp spines.

The three mullets (bottom: Thick-lipped grey mullet) have large lips, a large head that is flattened above, and pectoral fins situated high on the flanks. The first of the two dorsal fins is short, supported by four spines.

Also in the 'Know Your' series...

Know Your Bees
Thirty-two species of bees, each accompanied by their specific features, including details about their habitat, size and other relevant information
£4.99

Know Your Sheep
Forty-one breeds of sheep that can be seen on Britain's farms today
£4.99

Know Your Cats
Covers 42 breeds, each accompanied by a clear description covering the history, appearance and personality of the breed
£4.99

Know Your Goats
An illustrated guide to the identification of goats likely to be encountered in Britain today
£4.99

Know Your Dogs
Forty-five popular dog breeds from Dalmatians to Corgis. Each accompanied with text describing their history, characteristics and abilities
£4.99

Know Your Donkeys
An enchanting sample of 34 breeds of donkeys and mules from around the world, from the miniature to the mammoth
£4.99

Old Pond PUBLISHING

To order any of these titles please contact us at:
Tel: 0114 240 9930 • Email: contact@oldpond.com • www.oldpond.com
5m Enterprises Ltd., Benchmark House, 8 Smithy Wood Drive, Sheffield, S35 1QN